SNAKES

By Herbert S. Żim

Illustrated by James Gordon Irving

SCHOLASTIC BOOK SERVICES

NEW YORK • TORONTO • LONDON • AUCKLAND • SYDNEY • TOKYO

*Thanks are due to Dr. William H. Stickel,
United States Fish and Wildlife Service,
for reading and criticizing the manuscript.*

BLACK SNAKES
IN DEN

Copyright 1949 by Herbert S. Zimm. This edition is published by Scholastic Book Services, a division of Scholastic Magazines, Inc., by arrangement with William Morrow & Company.

10th printing . . . . January 1972

Printed in the U.S.A.

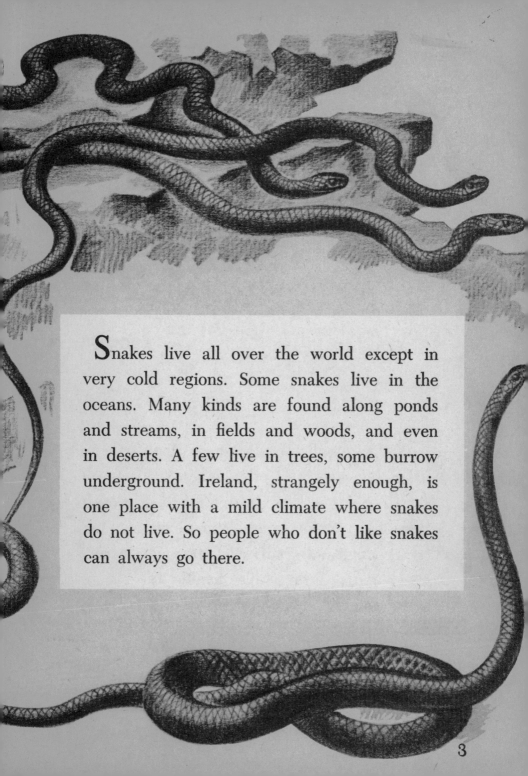

Snakes live all over the world except in very cold regions. Some snakes live in the oceans. Many kinds are found along ponds and streams, in fields and woods, and even in deserts. A few live in trees, some burrow underground. Ireland, strangely enough, is one place with a mild climate where snakes do not live. So people who don't like snakes can always go there.

DESERT TORTOISE 9½ IN.

THESE ARE

BOX
TURTLE
5½ IN.

CROCODILE 8 FT.

COMMON MILK SNAKE 30 IN.

In spite of all the odd stories about them, snakes live like most other animals. They are born. They grow. They search for food, protect themselves against their numerous enemies, have young, and finally die—the same as any other animals you could name. Yet snakes

REPTILES

ALLIGATOR 8 FT.

ADULT FIVE - LINED SKINK
9½ IN.

LIZARDS

LEOPARD LIZARD
12 IN.

sometimes act very differently from animals you commonly see. Snakes are more like lizards than any other kind of animal. Snakes and lizards, together with crocodiles, alligators, and turtles, make up the reptiles.

PTERANODON
SPREAD · 27 FT.

The dinosaurs that lived millions of years ago were reptiles too.

DIPLODOCUS
70 - 80 FT.

STEGOSAURUS

TYRANNOSAURUS
50 FT.

(DINOSAURS
ADAPTED
AFTER KNIGHT)

6

Before snakes are born, the male and female snakes mate, as other animals do, and the eggs begin to develop inside the female's body. Some female snakes lay from five to twelve or even more of these long eggs, covered with a tough, white, leathery skin. The snake lays her eggs in a hollow, rotted log, in dead leaves, or in warm soil, because the warmer the eggs are, the sooner they hatch. Unlike a bird, a female snake cannot warm her eggs enough to make much difference in their hatching.

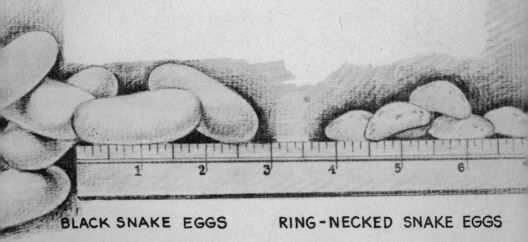

BLACK SNAKE EGGS   RING-NECKED SNAKE EGGS

Your body uses food to keep its temperature at about 99 degrees, day and night, summer and winter. The snake's temperature stays just about the same as the air around it. On a hot day a snake is hot; on a cool day it is cold. We call such animals "cold-blooded."

Some female snakes do stay curled around their eggs, but the heat for hatching them comes mostly from the rotting leaves and wood, or from the sun. The time it takes snake eggs to hatch depends partly on the weather and partly on the kind of snake. Some snake eggs hatch in about a week; others take twelve weeks or more.

The unborn snake grows a small "tooth" at the very tip of its head, to help cut through the tough covering of the egg. After the young snake has cut through, it pokes its head out and looks around. If it is frightened, it ducks right back again, and may take most of the day before it finally leaves the egg.

CHICKEN SNAKE

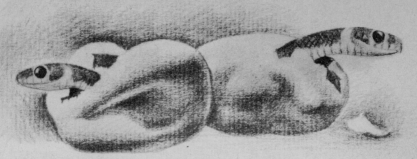

EGGS HATCHING
(RING - NECKED SNAKES)

Nearly half the snakes do not lay eggs at all. Their young remain in the body of the mother, each growing within a thin sack or membrane. When the snakes are born, this membrane tears and the young snakes break out. Snakes that are born alive and those that hatch from eggs are born about the same size— from four to fourteen inches long, depending on the kind of snake. Infant snakes are able to care for themselves. They can crawl, climb, and swim, catch food and eat. Once born, they are on their own. The mother pays no attention to them.

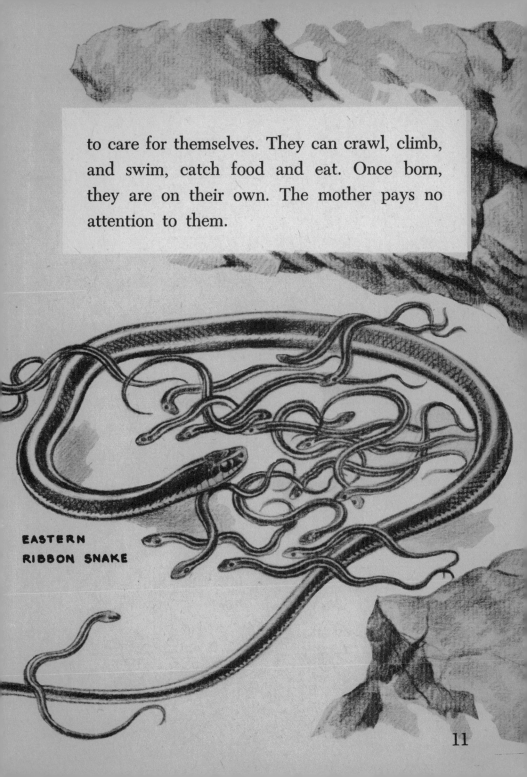

EASTERN
RIBBON SNAKE

At birth: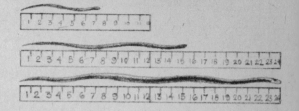

End of 1st year:

2nd to 3rd year:

GROWTH OF A COMMON GARTER SNAKE

If all goes well, a young snake will double its length during its first year. In two or three years it is full-grown or mature. At this age snakes instinctively seek a mate. After the male and female have mated, each usually goes its own way. After a time an egg-laying female lays its eggs. If the snake is the kind that bears its young alive, several months may pass before they are born.

Here are the more common American snakes. Some of them lay eggs and others have their young born alive.

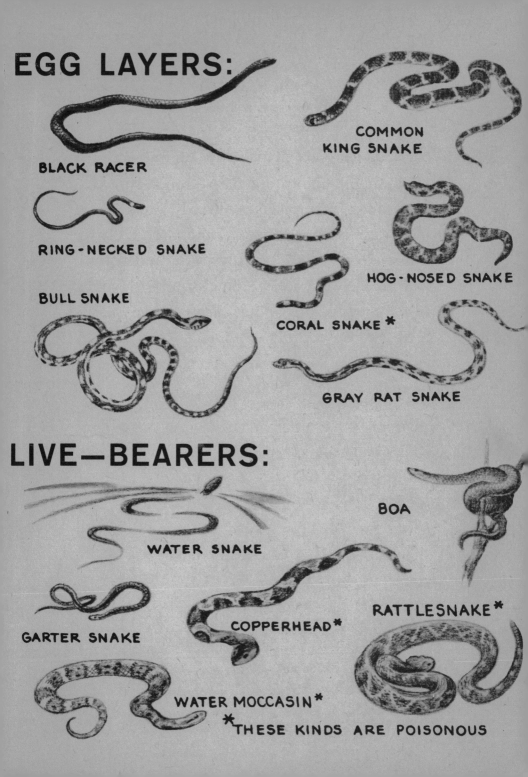

EGG LAYERS:

BLACK RACER

COMMON KING SNAKE

RING-NECKED SNAKE

BULL SNAKE

CORAL SNAKE *

HOG-NOSED SNAKE

GRAY RAT SNAKE

LIVE—BEARERS:

WATER SNAKE

BOA

GARTER SNAKE

COPPERHEAD *

RATTLESNAKE *

WATER MOCCASIN *

*THESE KINDS ARE POISONOUS

No snake eats plant food. All eat animals, from small rabbits down to ground-squirrels, rats, mice, other snakes, lizards, small birds and eggs, fish, frogs, worms, and insects. Garter snakes feed mainly on frogs, fish, and worms. Bull snakes eat rats, ground-squirrels, young rabbits, eggs, and young birds. Green snakes feed almost entirely on insects, and, as far as we know, so do many young snakes.

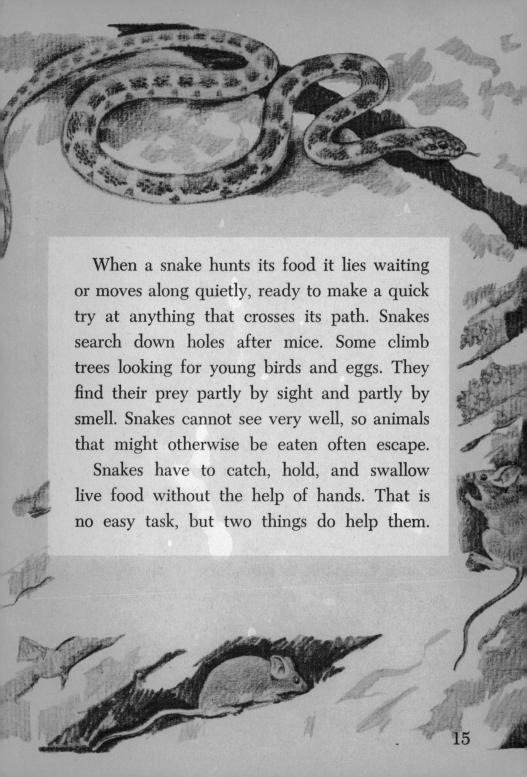

When a snake hunts its food it lies waiting or moves along quietly, ready to make a quick try at anything that crosses its path. Snakes search down holes after mice. Some climb trees looking for young birds and eggs. They find their prey partly by sight and partly by smell. Snakes cannot see very well, so animals that might otherwise be eaten often escape.

Snakes have to catch, hold, and swallow live food without the help of hands. That is no easy task, but two things do help them.

ROWS OF TEETH IN JAWS OF A NON POISONOUS SNAKE

Teeth are one. Snakes have rows of small, hooked teeth that run from the front to the back of the mouth. Most snakes have four rows on top, two on the bottom. These teeth slant toward the back of the snake's mouth, so once caught it is hard for any animal to escape. These teeth are no more poisonous than your own.

THE FLEXIBLE LIGAMENT
CONNECTING THE TWO
SEPARATE HALVES OF
A SNAKE'S LOWER JAW

The snake's jaws also help in feeding. They are not attached like the jawbone of other animals. A snake can open its mouth much wider than you think. Each side of the jaws can move separately, so a snake can hold an animal with one side of its mouth, while moving the other side to take a new grip. The snake's large mouth, elastic jaws, and a skin that stretches make it possible to swallow an animal so large that a considerable lump can be seen when the meal is over.

PINE SNAKE

EATING A RAT:

TAKING INTO MOUTH

SWALLOWING

SWALLOWING: TAIL ONLY SHOWS

AFTER SWALLOWING

EATING ANOTHER SNAKE

EATING
BIRD'S EGGS

EATING
A BIRD

SNAKES EATING

The snake digests food very much the way we do. It has a mouth, throat, stomach, liver, and intestines. Within a day after you have eaten, a heavy meal is completely digested. A snake may take four to six days or more to digest a meal. The juices in the snake's stomach and intestines are so strong that they can digest bones and skin. A snake's meal takes longer to digest and it lasts longer. Because snakes are cold-blooded, they use less energy in proportion to their size than do warm-blooded animals, and so they can get along with less food. Sometimes captive snakes eat only one meal a month and some have

CONSTRICTING

been known to go nearly two years without eating. Wild snakes often go for days or even weeks without food.

Since they are cold-blooded, snakes become slow and sluggish on cold days. In the fall, when the temperature begins to drop, snakes crawl into holes and cracks, or burrow into soil or under logs. There they remain inactive,

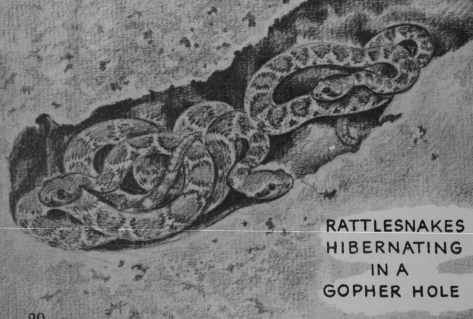

RATTLESNAKES HIBERNATING IN A GOPHER HOLE

hibernating till the following spring. Some snakes hibernate alone. Others gather together till there are a dozen or even a hundred or more in one place.

Warm-blooded animals have a cooling system to keep them from becoming too hot. When you perspire, you see that cooling system at work. Snakes haven't anything of the sort. They are as badly off when it is too hot as when it is too cold.

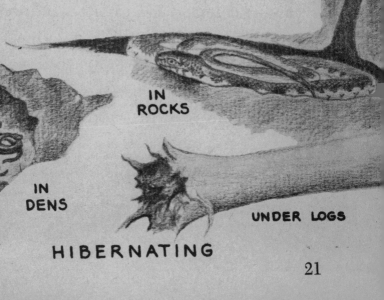

IN
ROCKS

IN
DENS

UNDER LOGS

HIBERNATING

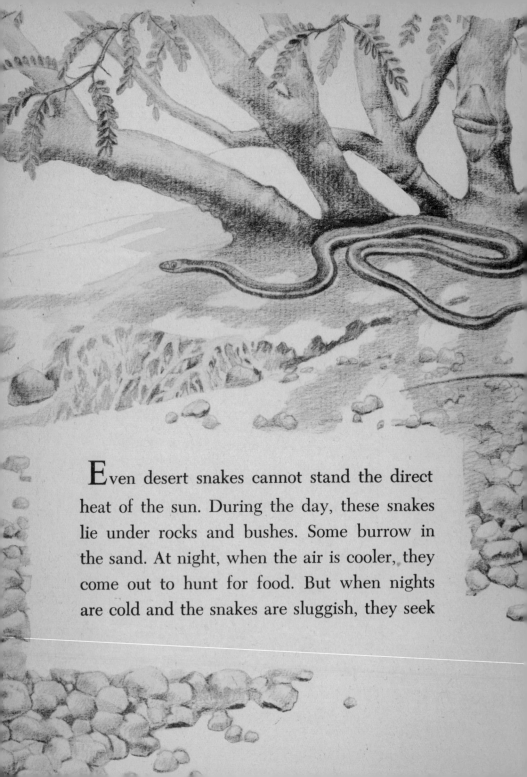

Even desert snakes cannot stand the direct heat of the sun. During the day, these snakes lie under rocks and bushes. Some burrow in the sand. At night, when the air is cooler, they come out to hunt for food. But when nights are cold and the snakes are sluggish, they seek out sun-warmed places in the daytime to take advantage of the heat. Millions of snakes are killed each year by automobiles because they find cement and asphalt roads warmer than the ground.

CALIFORNIA STRIPED RACER

People with mistaken ideas about snakes kill every snake they see. Some people kill snakes because they are afraid; others because they think all snakes are harmful. Snakes have many other enemies besides people. Animals like skunks and opossums dig up eggs and kill small snakes. Some hawks, owls, and eagles eat snakes regularly. An odd western bird, the road runner, feeds largely on lizards and small snakes. It will sometimes tackle and kill a large

ENEMIES OF

BROAD - WINGED
HAWK

ROADRUNNER

WEASEL

SNAKES

KING SNAKE

rattler. Finally, snakes eat each other. King, bull snakes, and racers, eat other snakes. And, if we can judge by other animals, many snakes are also killed by diseases.

Snakes have little protection against their enemies. Their best defense is to escape. A snake's movement for escape or for anything else is indeed curious. Snakes move in several ways. They can inch forward by a kind of walking on their ribs. This is interesting to watch and hard to describe. The underside of every snake is covered by a long row of scalelike plates. One edge of each plate is attached to the body at the end of each pair of ribs. The other edge overlaps the next plate in somewhat the same way as shingles on a roof. Muscles attached to the ribs and

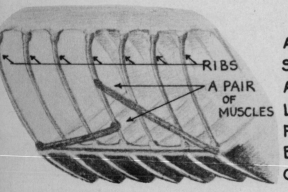

RIBS

A PAIR
OF
MUSCLES

A GREAT SERIES OF MUSCLES SIMILAR TO THIS PAIR CONTRAC ALTERNATELY TO LIFT THE LARGE VENTRAL SCALES FIRST FORWARD THEN BACKWARD. THIS MOVEMENT CARRIES THE SNAKE FORWARD

MOVEMENT OF A SNAKE

CORN SNAKE CROSSING FROM
ONE BRANCH TO ANOTHER

PINE SNAKE

RATTLESNAKE ON
ROCKY SURFACE

SNAKES MOVING

the plates enable the snake to move the plates backward a short distance. And moving the plates backward is the same as moving the snake forward. This peculiar inching movement starts near the snake's head and travels backward like a ripple, as the snake moves forward.

INDIGO SNAKE

More commonly snakes move ahead by a sort of side-to-side wiggle. This S-shaped movement permits them to push against the rough ground, pebbles, and grass, and thus move forward rapidly. They move so smoothly, so quietly, and so fast, they seem to disappear before your eyes. In grass or brush snakes take advantage of the support they can get, and use a combination of both types of movement.

The same thing happens when snakes climb. If a branch is steep, they will inch up. Or they may go faster, winding in and out of twigs and small branches. Only racers, rat snakes, and a few others do much climbing.

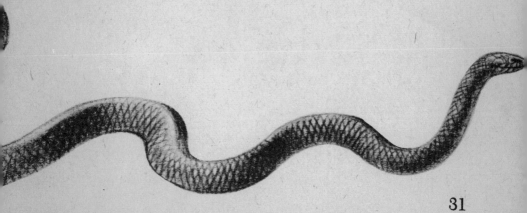

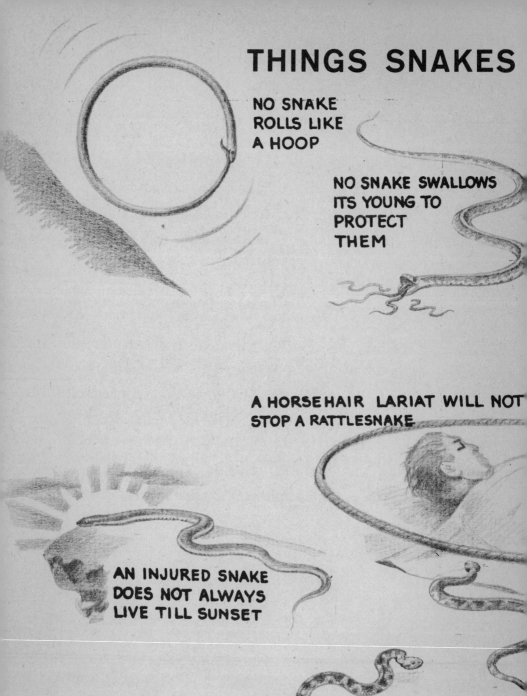

THINGS SNAKES

NO SNAKE ROLLS LIKE A HOOP

NO SNAKE SWALLOWS ITS YOUNG TO PROTECT THEM

A HORSEHAIR LARIAT WILL NOT STOP A RATTLESNAKE

AN INJURED SNAKE DOES NOT ALWAYS LIVE TILL SUNSET

DO <u>NOT</u> DO

MILK SNAKES
DO NOT
MILK COWS

SNAKES DO NOT
HYPNOTIZE THEIR PREY

SNAKES DO NOT
JUMP AT PEOPLE

SNAKES DO NOT
HAVE A
POISON STINGER
IN TAIL

Most snakes swim well, using a side-to-side wiggle. Water snakes and other kinds spend much of their life in and near water. No snakes in this country can jump, and stories about flying snakes turn out to be just one more kind of snake story. Most snakes cannot move much faster than a man walks—about four miles an hour. Some, like the racers, may go faster for short distances, if the ground is right.

A SNAKE CAN <u>NOT</u> RUN AS FAST AS A HORSE

Snakes have an added protection because
their colors and patterns blend so well with
the ground, rocks, and dead leaves. They also
can stay perfectly still so it is almost impossible
to see them unless you are right upon them.
A few snakes, when in danger, roll up like a
tight ball. Rattlers have a way of making an

RATTLING

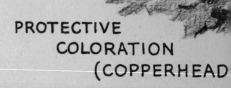

PROTECTIVE
COLORATION
(COPPERHEAD

HISSING

sSSS **PROTECTIVE**

unusual warning noise. Some other snakes that are not poisonous shake their tails back and forth rapidly in dry grass or leaves, making a noise like a rattler. Some produce a bad-smelling liquid from the glands at the base of their tails. Some, like the water snake, flatten themselves out and hiss. If they cannot escape, some snakes will strike, and some will bite.

VIBRATING TAIL
(PILOT BLACK SNAKE)

RUNNING AWAY

DEVICES

Small snakes like grass, ring-necked, ground, and sometimes garter snakes, often do nothing at all and may be picked up and handled by anyone.

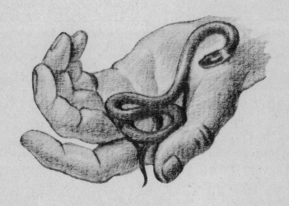

The hog-nosed snake (or puff adder, as it is sometimes called) is a harmless snake which, if cornered, will hiss, flatten, and then puff itself up. It acts ferocious and may even strike —but with its mouth tightly shut. As a last

HOG - NOSED SNAKE PLAYING DEAD

HOG - NOSED SNAKE

resort, it rolls over on its back and plays dead. After a while when things seem quiet, the hog-nosed snake will roll over again and go on its way. But if you turn the "dead" hog-nose over on its belly, it will promptly turn on its back again.

Finally, there are snakes which kill their prey and defend themselves by using poison. In some countries such snakes are extremely dangerous. In this country there is little reason for anyone being bitten by a snake and relatively few people are.

No other animals can make and store as much poison in their bodies as poisonous snakes can. Some snake poisons are much stronger than others. Copperhead and rattler poisons are relatively weak.

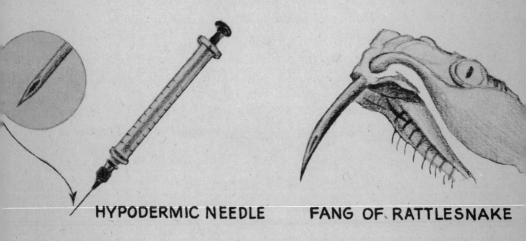

HYPODERMIC NEEDLE   FANG OF RATTLESNAKE

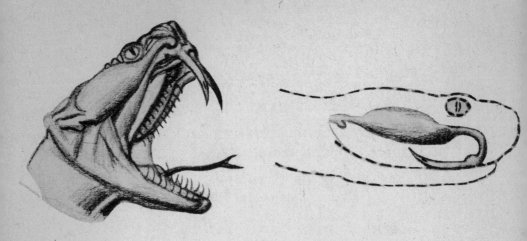

ERECT   DEPRESSED

A RATTLESNAKE'S FANGS

The poison—a pale yellow liquid—is made in two small sacs or glands in the snake's head, just beneath and behind the eyes. Two small tubes lead from the poison glands to the snake's mouth, where they join the fangs or hollow teeth. The fangs of our poisonous snakes are like the hollow needles a doctor uses to give injections. When a poisonous snake bites, its muscles automatically squeeze the poison sacs and the poison flows through the fangs into the wound.

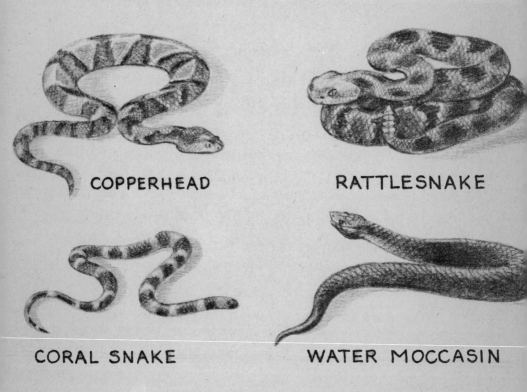

COPPERHEAD

RATTLESNAKE

CORAL SNAKE

WATER MOCCASIN

POISONOUS SNAKES

Poisonous snakes have an advantage in getting their food. Once a rattler strikes a rat or a gopher, there is little chance for its escape. The poison takes effect quickly because there is so much of it compared to the size of the animal. A human being is so much larger that the poison has less effect. It is unlikely for the bite of a rattler, copperhead, or moccasin to kill a grown person if help is given promptly. Doctors now have serums that are injected into anyone who has been bitten. Very prompt first aid is important. Avoiding poisonous snakes is best of all. Snake poison is only poisonous when injected. A rat

RESERVE FANGS OF RATTLESNAKE

1/100 OUNCE OF DRIED VENOM FROM AVERAGE SIZE RATTLESNAKE

killed by snake poison does not poison the snake which eats it. But if the rattler is bitten by another rattler (or accidentally by itself) it may die of snake poisoning.

1. APPLY TOURNIQUET SHORT DISTANCE ABOVE WOUND. (ANY STRIP OF CLOTH, SHOE-STRING CAN BE USED)

2. WITH STERILIZED KNIFE OR RAZOR BLADE MAKE INCISIONS ACROSS BITE. (MATCH FLAME WILL STERILIZE)

3. APPLY SUCTION TO INCISIONS. IF A SUCTION CUP IS NOT AVAILABLE USE MOUTH.

SEND FOR A DOCTO

KEEP PATIENT QUIET

FIRST AID FOR SNAKE BITE

TRIANGULAR SHAPED HEADS

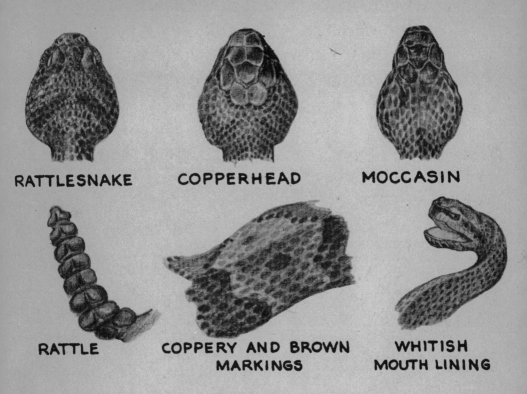

RATTLESNAKE   COPPERHEAD   MOCCASIN

RATTLE   COPPERY AND BROWN MARKINGS   WHITISH MOUTH LINING

Rattlers, copperheads, and moccasins are all pit vipers, poisonous snakes which can fold their fangs against the top of their mouths. They are the snakes with triangular-shaped heads, thick bodies, and thin necks. The brilliant-banded coral snake, a rarer and

CORAL SNAKE

even more poisonous snake of the South, has fangs which do not move. Both types of poisonous snakes have a number of extra fangs in reserve. If the working pair breaks, new ones quickly grow into place.

RATTLESNAKES

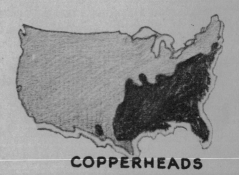

COPPERHEADS

THE RANGES OF

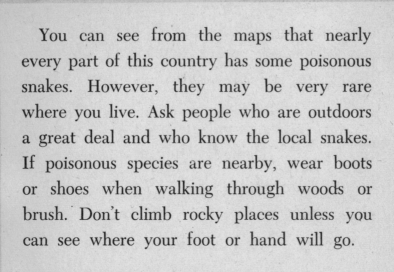

You can see from the maps that nearly every part of this country has some poisonous snakes. However, they may be very rare where you live. Ask people who are outdoors a great deal and who know the local snakes. If poisonous species are nearby, wear boots or shoes when walking through woods or brush. Don't climb rocky places unless you can see where your foot or hand will go.

MOCCASINS

CORAL SNAKES

POISONOUS SNAKES

People always want to know how big snakes grow and how long they live. The smallest snakes in this country are probably the worm and miter snakes, only eight to twelve inches long. Both are wormlike, and burrow underground. The size of large snakes is often exaggerated. The record seems to have been made by a pilot black snake nearly

MITER SNAKE

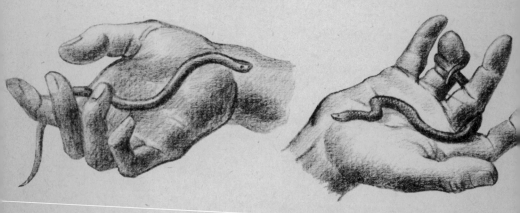

WORM SNAKE

SMALL SNAKES

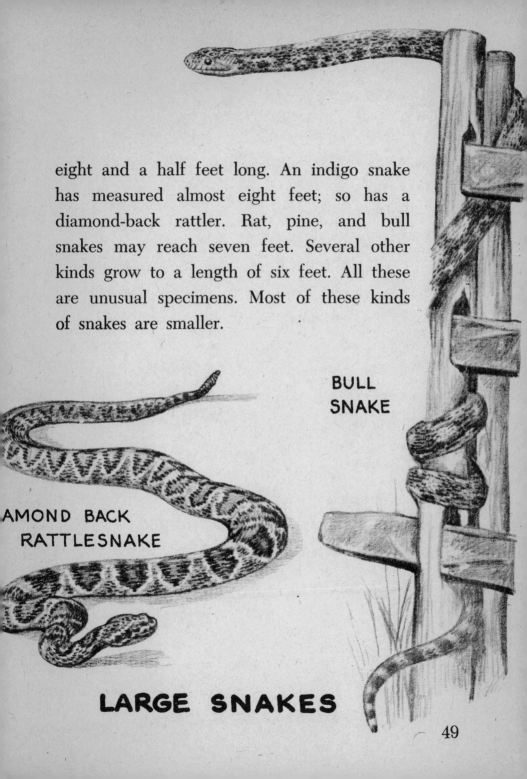

eight and a half feet long. An indigo snake has measured almost eight feet; so has a diamond-back rattler. Rat, pine, and bull snakes may reach seven feet. Several other kinds grow to a length of six feet. All these are unusual specimens. Most of these kinds of snakes are smaller.

BULL
SNAKE

AMOND BACK
RATTLESNAKE

LARGE SNAKES

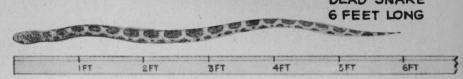

DEAD SNAKE
6 FEET LONG

1 FT   2 FT   3 FT   4 FT   5 FT   6 FT

Snakes grow like all other animals. The food they eat is digested and goes to build bones, muscle, skin, and blood. As you grow, you keep getting too big for your skin. As your old skin on the surface dies, new skin grows beneath it. Sometimes after a bath you can rub bits of this dead skin off. As a snake grows, its new skin grows too. But as the outer skin of a snake dies, it remains in one piece. The snake becomes duller. Its eyes become cloudy because they, too, are covered by this skin. Finally the snake rubs its nose against a rock till it loosens the dead skin

SKIN OF SAME SNAKE
ON DRYING BOARD

1FT   2FT   3FT   4FT   5FT   6FT

there. Then it begins to move forward and slowly rubs its way out of its skin, leaving the shed skin inside out behind it. Perhaps you have found such snake skins yourself. A snake may shed a number of times during the summer if it is eating well and growing fast.

CRESTED FLYCATCHER
OFTEN USES A CAST SKIN
IN NEST BUILDING

FRAGMENTARY SKIN (INSIDE OUT)
SHOWING EYE COVERING

A NEARLY COMPLETE CAST
SKIN (INSIDE OUT)

No one knows how long snakes may live. A few captive snakes have survived more than twenty years, but the chances are that wild snakes do not escape hunger, disease, and enemies for even half that long. However, one thing is giving wild snakes a longer life. Scientists have convinced us that many kinds of snakes are valuable to the farmer because they feed largely on rats and mice. Other

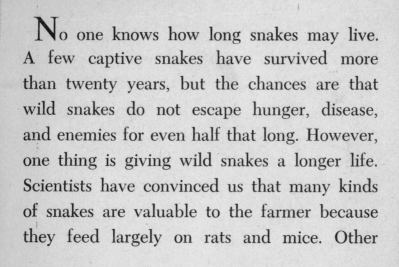

snakes that are not of direct value do no real harm and should be given as much chance to survive as other wild creatures. People are learning not to kill snakes except for occasional poisonous ones found where they might be dangerous.

Some people keep snakes as pets even though they are not very intelligent or active. If you want to have a snake for a pet, find out first whether any poisonous kinds may be found in the vicinity. Then make sure you can identify a poisonous one. If you are in doubt, leave them alone. Look for snakes

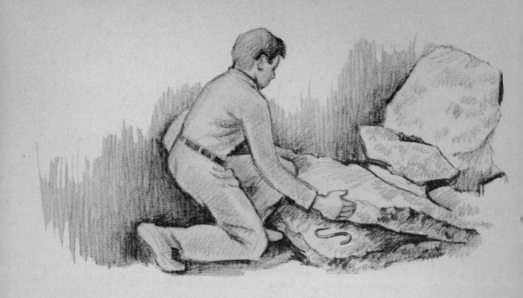

in fields, open woods, and along streams. Turn over rocks and old logs. Move quietly because snakes can feel the vibrations as you walk. If you do find a snake and are sure it is not poisonous, grab it right back of the head, since that will keep it from biting.

Some snakes are tame enough to pick up and handle immediately. Others tame down after they have been handled a while. When you hold a snake, support its body by letting it lie partly on your hands or arm. Some snakes are unhappy in captivity. If they do not tame easily, it is best to let them go.

HOLDING
A TAME SNAKE

RIGHT
WAY

WRONG
WAY

Any simple wooden box will do to house a pet snake. Equip the box with a sliding glass front and a dozen small ventilation holes around the sides and you have a fine cage. Snakes do not need much room. A cage about ten inches wide, twenty-four inches long, and ten inches high is fine for most medium-sized snakes. A heavy glass dish two or three inches deep, half filled with water, does for drinking and bathing. A rock or branch to crawl over and a sprinkling of sand on the floor are all the furnishings you need.

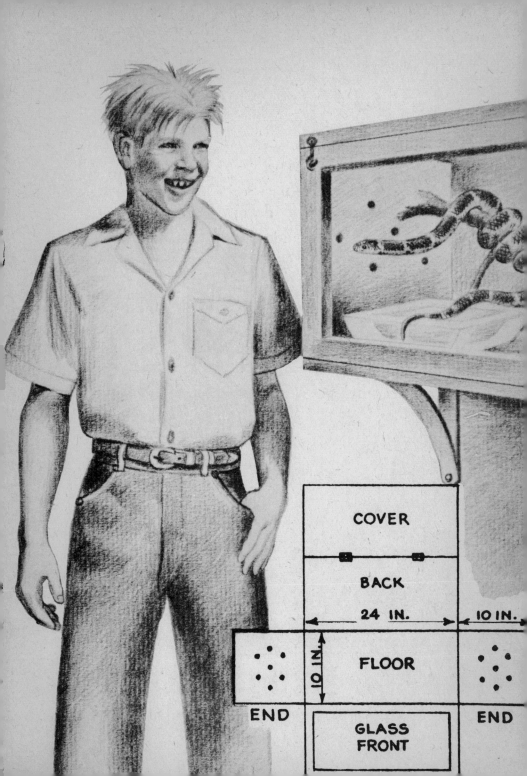

COVER

BACK

24 IN.

10 IN.

10 IN.

FLOOR

END

END

GLASS
FRONT

Feeding a pet snake is a problem, for snakes eat live food and some will not eat in captivity. Earthworms are good food for some small snakes, frogs for some medium-sized kinds. Racers, milk, bull, rat, and king snakes often eat mice.

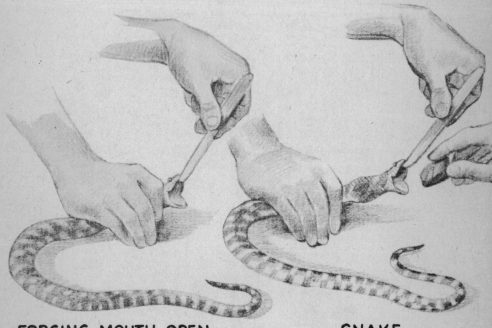

FORCING MOUTH OPEN
WITH BLUNT INSTRUMENT

SNAKE
SWALLOWING

FORCE-FEEDING PET SNAKE

A snake that eats well during the warm months may go through the winter without food, even though it does not hibernate. Sometimes a snake can be trained to eat small pieces of meat or fish if they are wiggled in front of its nose or pushed into its mouth.

SNAKE EATING OF
OWN ACCORD

Well-fed snakes in dry cages are likely to stay healthy. Some may develop skin infections if the floor of the cage is wet. Wash any sore spots in a mild germ-killing solution. When a snake gets ill, it's usually best to turn it loose.

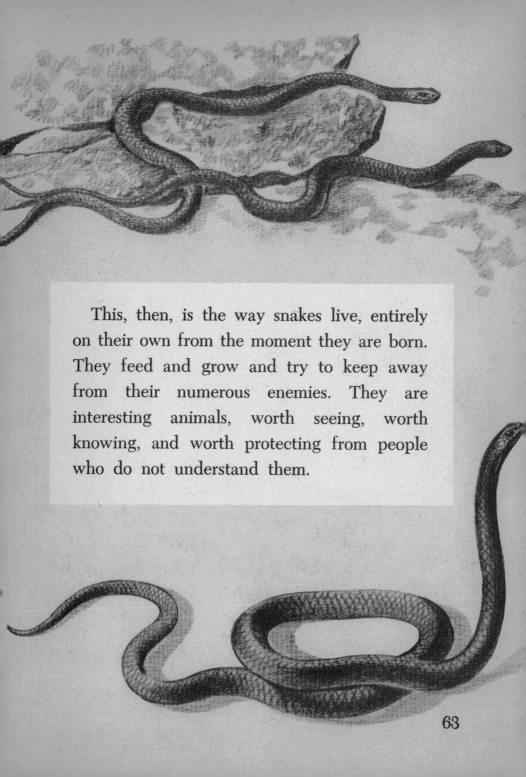

This, then, is the way snakes live, entirely on their own from the moment they are born. They feed and grow and try to keep away from their numerous enemies. They are interesting animals, worth seeing, worth knowing, and worth protecting from people who do not understand them.